A+ books

Bilingual Picture Dictionaries

# My First Book of
# Spanish Words

by Katy R. Kudela

Translator: Translations.com

Capstone press®

Mankato, Minnesota

apple
**la manzana**
(mahn-SAH-nah)

# Table of Contents

# How to Use This Dictionary

This book is full of useful words in both Spanish and English. The English word appears first, followed by the Spanish word. Look below each Spanish word for help to sound it out. Try reading the words aloud.

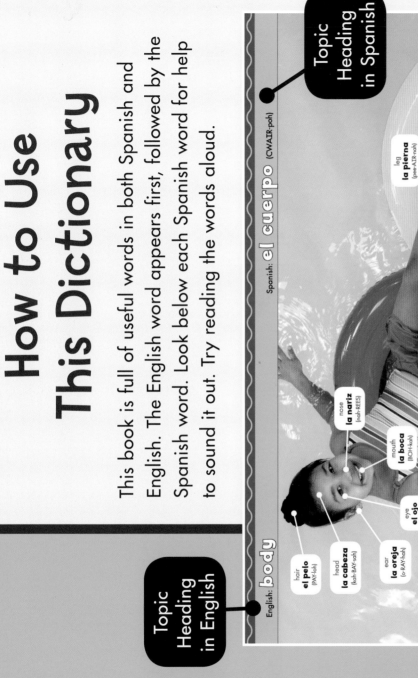

English: **body**

Spanish: **el cuerpo** (CWAIR-poh)

hair
**el pelo**
(PAY-loh)

head
**la cabeza**
(kah-BAY-sah)

ear
**la oreja**
(o-RAY-hah)

nose
**la nariz**
(nah-REES)

mouth
**la boca**
(BOH-kah)

eye
**el ojo**
(OH-hoh)

arm
**el brazo**
(BRAH-soh)

hand
**la mano**
(MAH-noh)

leg
**la pierna**
(pee-AIR-nah)

foot
**el pie**
(pee-AY)

Topic Heading in English

Topic Heading in Spanish

Word in English
**Word in Spanish**
(pronunciation)

Notes about the Spanish Language
The Spanish language usually includes "el," "la," "los," and "las" before nouns. These all mean "the" in Spanish. The pronunciations for these articles are below.

**el** (ehl)    **los** (lohs)
**la** (lah)    **las** (lahs)

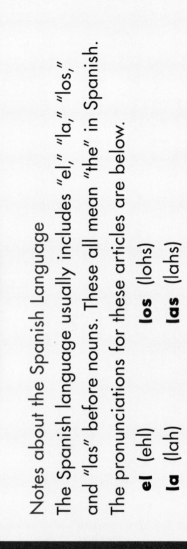

4

aunt
**la tía**
(TEE-ah)

uncle
**el tío**
(TEE-oh)

cousin
**el primo**
(PREE-moh)

baby
**el bebé**
(bay-BAY)

mother
**la mamá**
(mah-MAH)

Spanish: **la familia** (fah-MEE-lee-ah)

father
**el papá** (pah-PAH)

sister
**la hermana** (air-MAH-nah)

grandmother
**la abuela** (ah-BWAY-lah)

grandfather
**el abuelo** (ah-BWAY-loh)

brother
**el hermano** (air-MAH-noh)

5

hair
**el pelo**
(PAY-loh)

head
**la cabeza**
(kah-BAY-sah)

ear
**la oreja**
(o-RAY-hah)

arm
**el brazo**
(BRAH-soh)

hand
**la mano**
(MAH-noh)

eye
**el ojo**
(OH-hoh)

mouth
**la boca**
(BOH-kah)

nose
**la nariz**
(nah-REES)

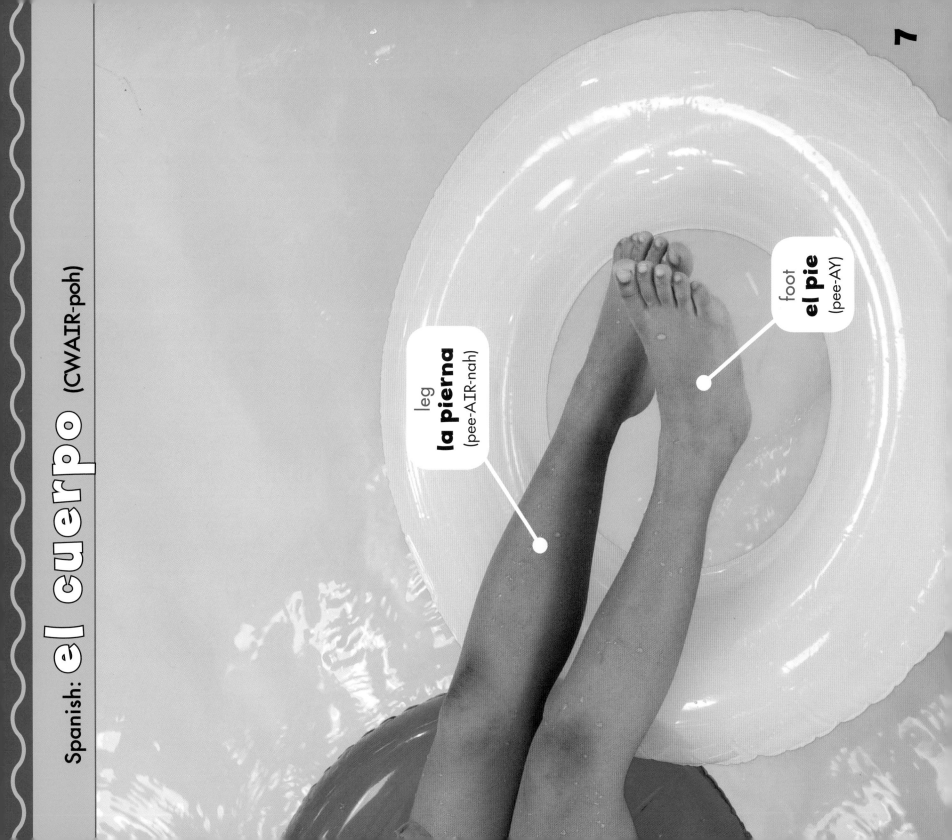

Spanish: **el cuerpo** (CWAIR-poh)

leg
**la pierna** (pee-AIR-nah)

foot
**el pie** (pee-AY)

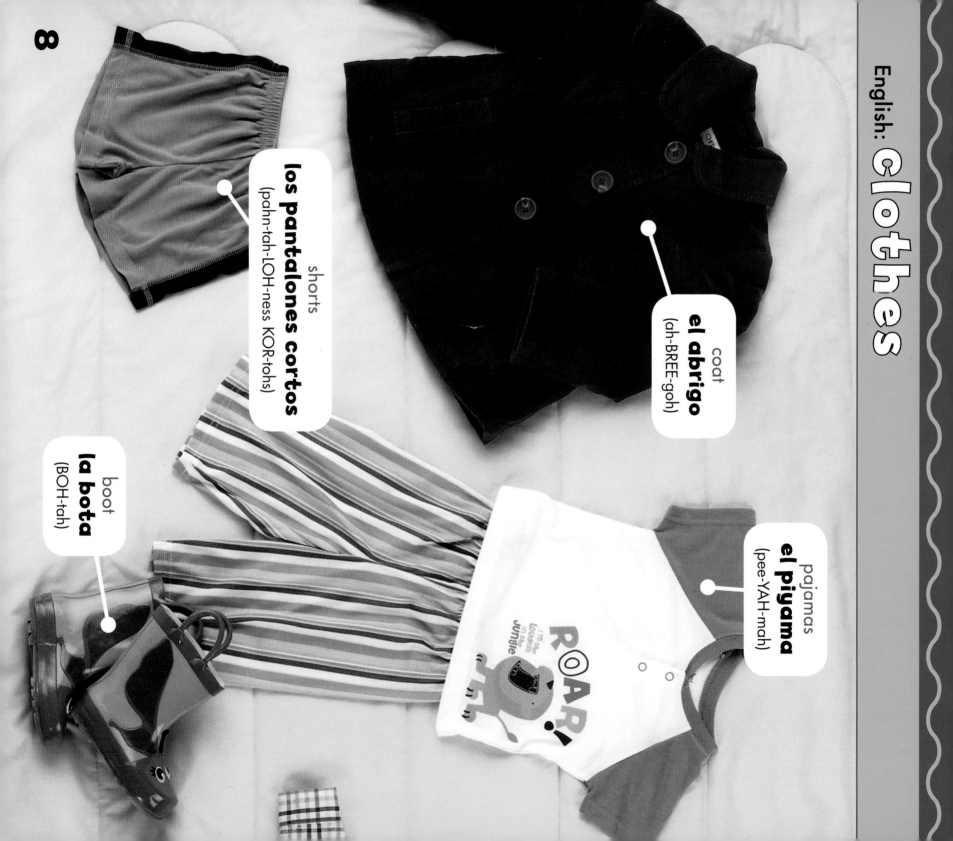

shorts
**los pantalones cortos**
(pahn-tah-LOH-ness KOR-tohs)

coat
**el abrigo**
(ah-BREE-goh)

boot
**la bota**
(BOH-tah)

pajamas
**el piyama**
(pee-YAH-mah)

Spanish: **la ropa** (ROH-pah)

shoe
**el zapato** (sah-PAH-toh)

pants
**los pantalones** (pahn-tah-LOH-ness)

dress
**el vestido** (ves-TEE-doh)

sock
**el calcetín** (kal-say-TEEN)

shirt
**la camisa** (kah-MEE-sah)

hat
**el sombrero** (sohm-BRAY-roh)

10

kite
**la cometa**
(koh-MAY-tah)

puzzle
**el rompecabezas**
(rohm-pay-kah-BAY-sahs)

train
**el tren**
(trayn)

wagon
**el carro**
(KAHR-roh)

doll
**la muñeca**
(moo-NYAY-kah)

Spanish: **los juguetes** (hoo-GAY-tays)

puppet
**el títere** (TEE-tay-ray)

ball
**la pelota** (pay-LOH-tah)

skateboard
**la patineta** (pah-tee-NAY-tah)

bat
**el bate** (BAH-tay)

jump rope
**la cuerda de saltar** (KWAIR-dah day sahl-TAHR)

window
**la ventana**
(ven-TAH-nah)

curtain
**la cortina**
(kor-TEE-nah)

blanket
**la sábana**
(SAH-bah-nah)

dresser
**el tocador**
(toh-kah-DOR)

picture
**el cuadro**
(KWAH-droh)

lamp
**la lámpara**
(LAHM-pah-rah)

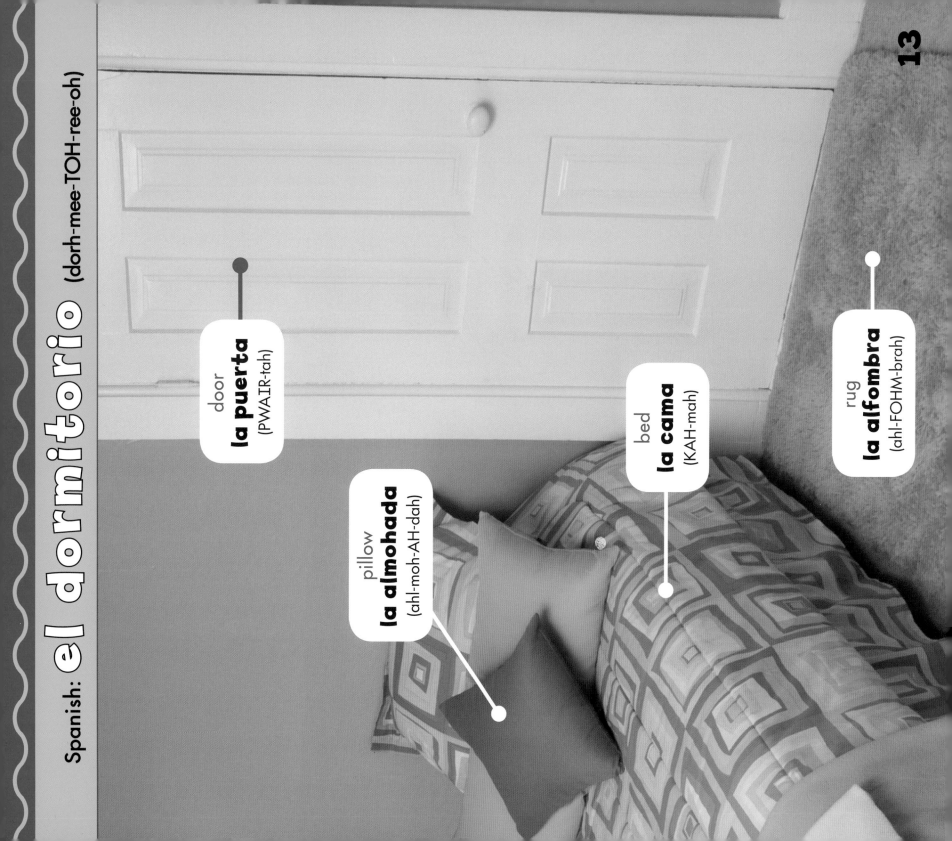

Spanish: **el dormitorio** (dorh-mee-TOH-ree-oh)

door
**la puerta** (PWAIR-tah)

pillow
**la almohada** (ahl-moh-AH-dah)

bed
**la cama** (KAH-mah)

rug
**la alfombra** (ahl-FOHM-brah)

toilet
**el inodoro**
(in-oh-DOH-roh)

soap
**el jabón**
(hah-BONE)

bathtub
**la bañera**
(bah-NYAY-rah)

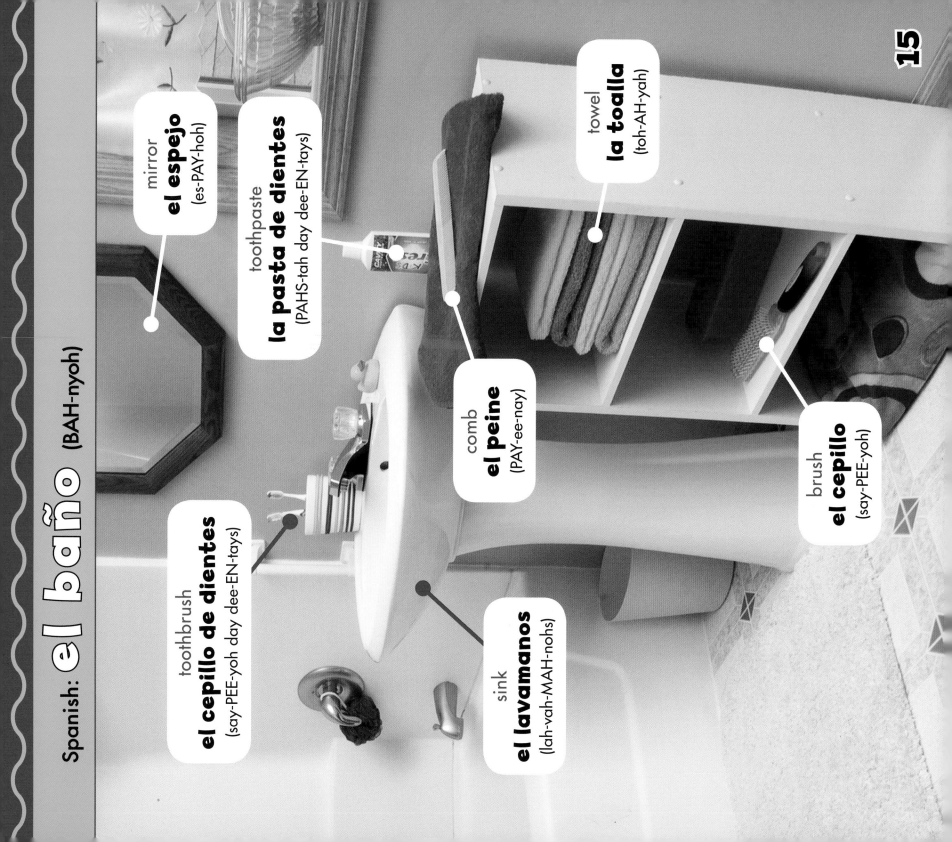

Spanish: **el baño** (BAH-nyoh)

mirror
**el espejo**
(es-PAY-hoh)

toothpaste
**la pasta de dientes**
(PAHS-tah day dee-EN-tays)

towel
**la toalla**
(toh-AH-yah)

comb
**el peine**
(PAY-ee-nay)

brush
**el cepillo**
(say-PEE-yoh)

toothbrush
**el cepillo de dientes**
(say-PEE-yoh day dee-EN-tays)

sink
**el lavamanos**
(lah-vah-MAH-nohs)

bowl
**el tazón**
(tah-SONE)

stove
**la estufa**
(es-TOO-fah)

oven
**el horno**
(OR-noh)

pot
**la olla**
(OY-yah)

Spanish: **la cocina** (ko-SEE-nah)

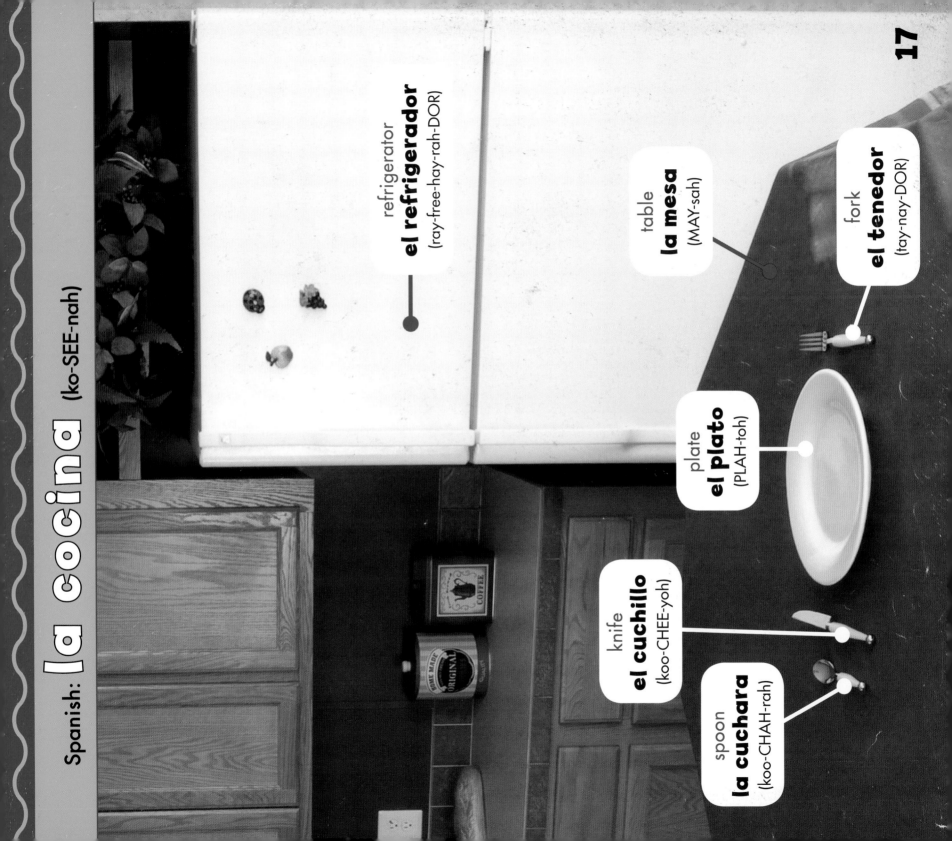

refrigerator
**el refrigerador**
(ray-free-hay-rah-DOR)

table
**la mesa**
(MAY-sah)

fork
**el tenedor**
(tay-nay-DOR)

plate
**el plato**
(PLAH-toh)

knife
**el cuchillo**
(koo-CHEE-yoh)

spoon
**la cuchara**
(koo-CHAH-rah)

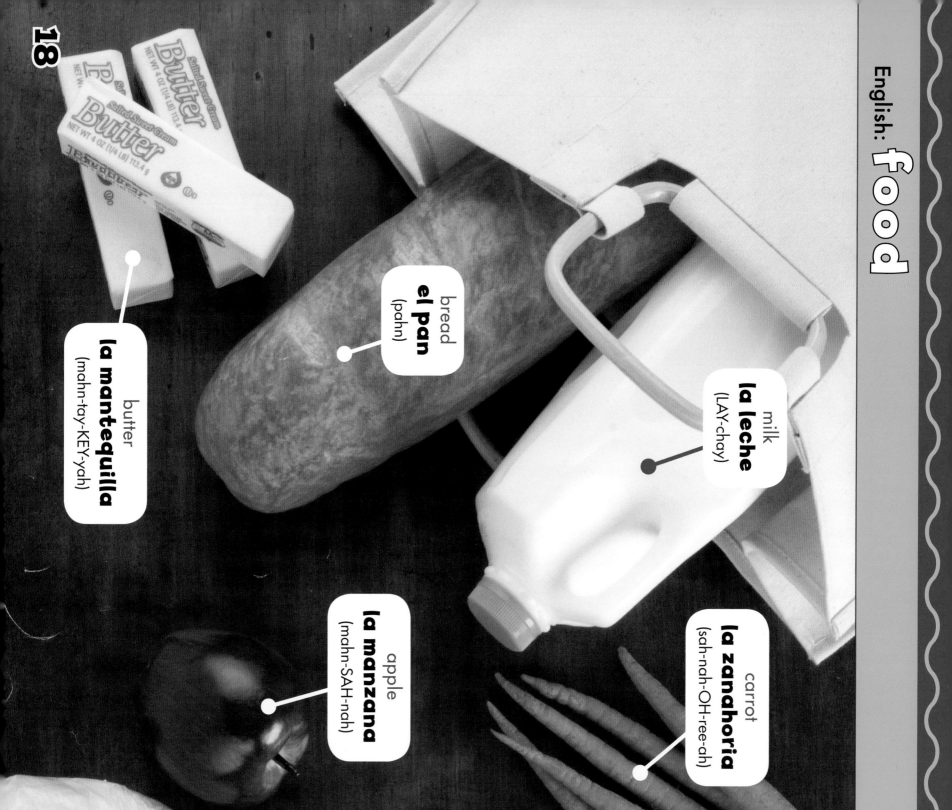

butter
**la mantequilla**
(mahn-tay-KEY-yah)

bread
**el pan**
(pahn)

milk
**la leche**
(LAY-chay)

apple
**la manzana**
(mahn-SAH-nah)

carrot
**la zanahoria**
(sah-nah-OH-ree-ah)

Spanish: la comida (ko-MEE-dah)

egg
**el huevo** (WAY-voh)

pea
**la arveja** (ar-VAY-hah)

orange
**la naranja** (nah-RAHN-hah)

sandwich
**el sándwich** (SAHND-weech)

rice
**el arroz** (ahr-ROHS)

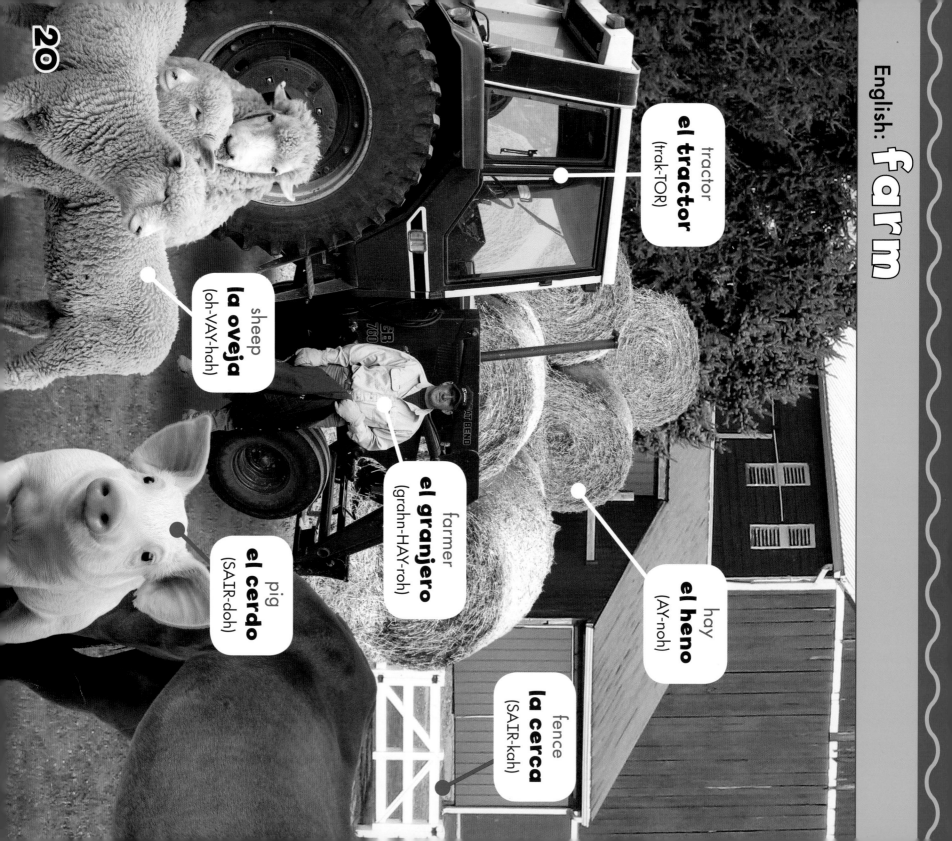

tractor
**el tractor**
(trak-TOR)

sheep
**la oveja**
(oh-VAY-hah)

farmer
**el granjero**
(grahn-HAY-roh)

pig
**el cerdo**
(SAIR-doh)

hay
**el heno**
(AY-noh)

fence
**la cerca**
(SAIR-kah)

English: **garden**

leaf
**la hoja**
(OH-hah)

shovel
**la pala**
(PAH-lah)

worm
**la lombriz**
(lom-BREES)

bird
**el pájaro**
(PAH-hah-roh)

flower
**la flor**
(flor)

butterfly
**la mariposa**
(mah-ree-POH-sah)

Spanish: **el jardín** (har-DEEN)

plant
**la planta** (PLAHN-tah)

grass
**el césped** (SES-pehd)

seed
**la semilla** (say-MEE-yah)

dirt
**la tierra** (tee-AIR-rah)

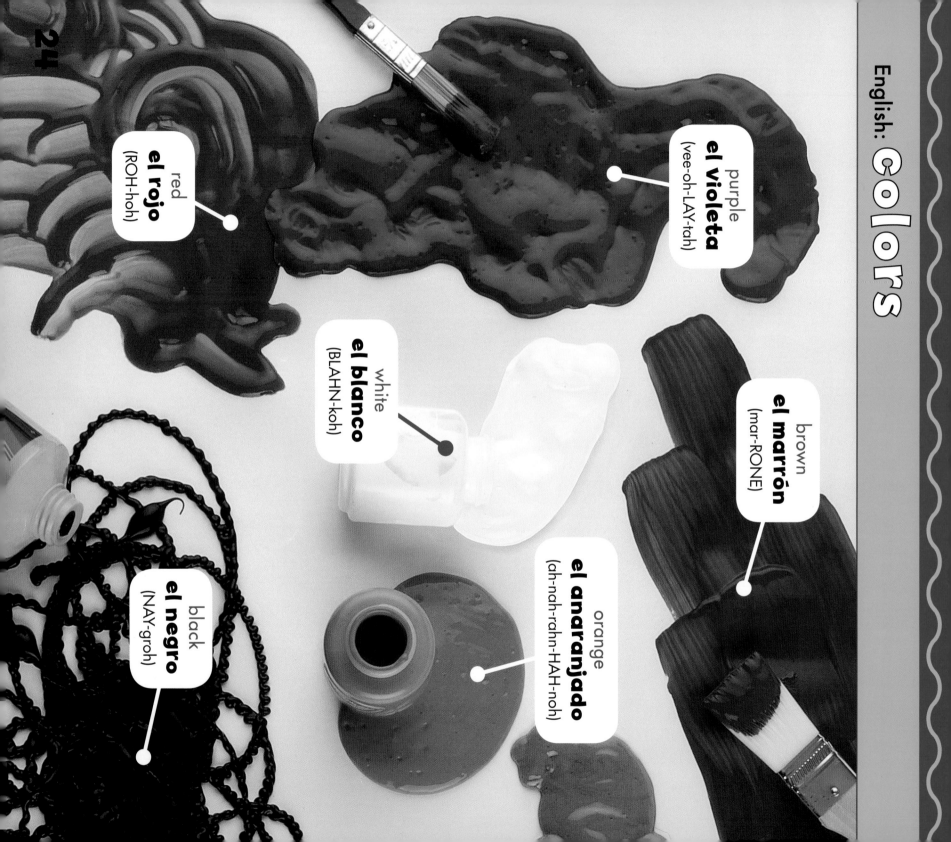

red
**el rojo**
(ROH-hoh)

purple
**el violeta**
(vee-oh-LAY-tah)

white
**el blanco**
(BLAHN-koh)

brown
**el marrón**
(mar-RONE)

black
**el negro**
(NAY-groh)

orange
**el anaranjado**
(ah-nah-rahn-HAH-noh)

Spanish: **los colores** (koh-LOHR-es)

blue
**el azul** (ah-SOOL)

green
**el verde** (VAIR-day)

pink
**el rosado** (roh-SAH-doh)

yellow
**el amarillo** (ah-mah-REE-yoh)

English: **Classroom**

book
**el libro**
(LEE-broh)

teacher
**la maestra**
(mah-ES-trah)

desk
**el escritorio**
(es-kree-TOH-ree-oh)

pencil
**el lápiz**
(LAH-pees)

crayon
**el crayón**
(krah-YONE)

Spanish: el aula (AH-oo-lah)

map
**el mapa**
(MAH-pah)

paper
**el papel**
(pah-PEHL)

computer
**la computadora**
(kohm-poo-tah-DOR-rah)

clock
**el reloj**
(ray-LOH)

chair
**la silla**
(SEE-yah)

English: **city**

bicycle
**la bicicleta**
(bee-see-KLAY-tah)

car
**el automóvil**
(ow-toh-MOH-veel)

store
**la tienda**
(tee-EN-dah)

traffic light
**el semáforo**
(say-MAH-for-oh)

library
**la biblioteca**
(bee-blee-oh-TAY-kah)

ONE WAY

Tuesday 2:00-5:00
Thursday 2:00-6:00

LIBRARY

# Spanish: la ciudad (see-oo-DAHD)

bus
**el autobús** (ow-toh-BOOS)

sign
**la señal** (seh-NYAHL)

tree
**el árbol** (AR-bol)

park
**el parque** (PAR-kay)

street
**la calle** (KAH-yay)

STOP

## Numbers • **Los números** (NOO-may-rohs)

1. one • **el uno** (OO-noh)
2. two • **el dos** (dose)
3. three • **el tres** (trays)
4. four • **el cuatro** (KWAH-troh)
5. five • **el cinco** (SEEN-koh)
6. six • **el seis** (SAY-ees)
7. seven • **el siete** (see-AY-tay)
8. eight • **el ocho** (OH-choh)
9. nine • **el nueve** (noo-AY-vay)
10. ten • **el diez** (dee-EHS)

## Useful Phrases • **Frases útiles** (FRAH-ses OO-teel-es)

yes • **sí** (see)

no • **no** (noh)

hello • **hola** (OH-lah)

good-bye • **adiós** (ah-dee-OHS)

good morning • **buenos días** (BWEN-ohs DEE-ahs)

good night • **buenas noches** (BWEN-ahs NOH-chays)

please • **por favor** (por fah-VOR)

thank you • **gracias** (GRAH-see-ahs)

excuse me • **permiso** (pair-MEE-soh)

My name is _____. • **Me llamo** _____. (may YAH-moh)

# Read More

*DK First Spanish Picture Dictionary.* New York: Dorling Kindersley, 2005.

**Emberley, Rebecca.** *My Big Book of Spanish Words.* New York: LB Kids, 2008.

*Vox First Spanish Picture Dictionary.* Chicago: McGraw-Hill, 2004.

# Internet Sites

FactHound offers a safe, fun way to find Internet sites related to this book. All of the sites on FactHound have been researched by our staff.

Here's all you do:

Visit *www.facthound.com*

FactHound will fetch the best sites for you!

A+ Books are published by Capstone Press,
151 Good Counsel Drive, P.O. Box 669, Mankato, Minnesota 56002.
www.capstonepub.com

Printed in the United States of America in North Mankato, Minnesota.

*Library of Congress Cataloging-in-Publication Data*
Kudela, Katy R.
  My first book of Spanish words / by Katy R. Kudela.
    p. cm. — (A+ books. Bilingual picture dictionaries)
  Summary: "Simple text paired with themed photos invite the reader to learn to speak
Spanish" — Provided by publisher.
  Includes bibliographical references.
  ISBN 978-1-4296-3298-0 (library binding)
  ISBN 978-1-4296-3852-4 (paperback)
  1. Picture dictionaries, Spanish — Juvenile literature. 2. Picture dictionaries,
English — Juvenile literature. 3. Spanish language — Dictionaries, Juvenile — English.
4. English language — Dictionaries, Juven le — Spanish. I. Title. II. Series.
PC4629.K83 2010
463'.21 — dc22
                                        2009005518

## Credits

Juliette Peters, designer; Wanda Winch, media researcher

### Photo Credits

Capstone Press/Gary Sundermeyer, cover (pig), 20 (farmer with tractor, pig)
Capstone Press/Karon Dubke, cover (ball, sock), back cover (toothbrush, apple), 1, 3,
  4–5, 6–7, 8–9, 10–11, 12–13, 14–15, 16–17, 18–19, 22–23, 24–25, 26–27
Image Farm, back cover, 1, 2, 31, 32 (design elements)
iStockphoto/Andrew Gentry, 28 (main street)
Photodisc, cover (flower)
Shutterstock/Adrian Matthiassen, cover (butterfly); David Hughes, 20 (hay); Eric Isselee,
  20–21 (horse); hamurishi, 28 (bike); Jim Mills, 29 (stop sign); Kelli Westfal, 28
  (traffic light); Levgeniia Tikhonova, 2 (chickens); Margo Harrison, 20 (sheep);
  MaxPhoto, 21 (cow and calf); Melinda Fawver, 29 (bus); Robert Elias, 20–21
  (barn, fence); Vladimir Mucibabic, 28–29 (city skyline)

## Note to Parents, Teachers, and Librarians

Learning to speak a second language at a young age has been shown to improve overall
academic performance, boost problem-solving ability, and foster an appreciation for other
cultures. Early exposure to language skills provides a strong foundation for other subject
areas, including math and reasoning. Introducing children to a second language can help to
lay the groundwork for future academic success and cultural awareness.

022010
005713R